Why it works
Electricity

Anna Claybourne

QEB

QEB Publishing

Author Anna Claybourne
Consultant Terry Jennings
Editor Louisa Somerville
Designer Susi Martin
Picture Researcher Claudia Tate
Illustrator John Haslam
Photographer Michael Wicks

Publisher Steve Evans
Creative Director Zeta Davies

Picture credits
Corbis 5
Getty 14
Shutterstock 4, 5, 6, 7, 8, 9, 10, 11, 12, 13, 15, 16, 17, 19, 20, 21

Published in the United States by
QEB Publishing, Inc.
23062 La Cadena Drive
Laguna Hills, CA 92653

www.qeb-publishing.com

Library of Congress Control Number: 2008011708

ISBN 978 1 59566 559 1

Printed and bound in the United States

Words in **bold** can be found in the glossary on page 22.

Contents

Electric world

Look around you. What can you see that runs on electricity? Most of us use electrical things every day.

We use electric lights to light our houses. Street lamps and traffic lights are electric as well.

Electric lights in buildings and outside in the street allow us to see after dark.

Radios and televisions run on electricity. You probably play with electric toys and computer games, too.

Electricity helps to make life easier. There are electric trains, cars, and buses. We use electric telephones.

Electric **appliances** make cooking and cleaning easier.

WARNING!
Never play with electrical **sockets**. The electricity supply can be very dangerous and you could harm yourself badly.

What does electricity do?

Electricity is a kind of **energy**. Energy makes things work. Electrical appliances turn electricity into other kinds of energy, such as heat, sound, light, or movement.

Television

computer

Iron

Food processor

Make a list of electrical appliances that you and your family use at home. Do you use all the things on these two pages?

A bedside lamp turns electricity into light energy.

An electric fan has a blade that spins round very fast to make a breeze.

Fan

One kind of electricity is called **electric current**. It comes from a power station. Appliances in your house plug into the electric current through wires in the walls.

Hair dryer

A hair dryer turns electricity into heat, sound, and movement energy.

Toaster

A toaster turns electricity into heat to toast bread.

Where is our electricity from?

Most of the electricity we use comes from big buildings called power stations. A power station changes the energy in coal, oil, or gas into electricity.

The electricity goes along thick wires. These hang on tall towers called pylons. Thinner wires take the electricity to the sockets in our homes. Then we can use it.

We plug appliances, such as kettles and lamps, into the sockets to connect them to the electricity supply.

Pylons carry electricity along thick wires to our homes.

Electricity can also come from other forms of energy, such as wind or moving water.

This power station turns energy from moving water into electricity.

A wind **turbine** turns energy from the wind into electricity.

Making a circuit

Terminals

An electrical circuit is a loop that electricity can flow around. You can make one using sticky tape, a small **battery,** and two pieces of electrical wire from a hardware store.

A 9-volt battery is the easiest to use. Every battery has two **terminals**.

9-volt battery

Electrical wires are usually made of a metal called copper, which is then coated with plastic.

Ask an adult to cut some of the plastic off both ends of each wire.

Copper wire

Plastic coating

Make sure each wire only touches one terminal.

Try this

1 Twist the bare end of one wire around a terminal, like this. Fix it in place with sticky tape.

2 Twist the other wire around in a loop and fix it to the other terminal using sticky tape.

3 To make a circuit, touch the loose ends of the wires together. Electricity will flow around the circuit.

It's a fact

The wires link one terminal of the battery to the other. This makes a loop that electricity from the battery can flow around.

Electric light

Bulb

Now you have made a circuit, you can use it to power a lightbulb. You will need a small bulb and a bulb holder. You can buy them at a hardware or model store.

The bulb holder has two **contacts**.

Try this

1 Carefully screw the lightbulb into the inside of the bulb holder.

Each wire is still attached to a terminal.

2 Take the two free ends of the wires in your circuit. Touch them to the two contacts of the bulb holder.

Contact

Contact

Bulb holder

12

It's a fact

Electricity now flows around the circuit and through the bulb, making it glow.

A bulb has a very thin wire in it, called a filament. Electricity in the filament makes it get hot and glow.

Filament

Many people use low-energy lightbulbs in their homes. These bulbs use less electricity than ordinary lightbulbs, and last much longer.

LIGHT LOOPS

Electric lights in your home also work on a circuit. Electricity flows around the circuit, and through the lightbulb.

13

Switching on and off

You turn most electrical appliances on and off with a **switch**. To turn the appliance on, the switch connects the wires in a circuit together. Electricity flows and makes the appliance work. You can see how this works with your circuit.

The bulb is off.

Wire ·····

Contact

Try this

Switch the lightbulb on and off by just moving one wire on and off the contact.

When you move the wire away, you break the loop. The light goes out.

A light switch on the wall is part of a big circuit inside the walls of a building. It makes a loop linking the light to the electricity supply.

You press a switch to turn a hair dryer on and off. Pressing the switch off breaks the circuit. Pressing the switch on connects the wires again.

WARNING! Never touch electrical switches with wet hands. Electricity can flow through water and give you a very harmful shock.

Sticky electricity

Static electricity is another kind of electricity. Unlike electric current, which flows through wires, static electricity collects in an object, such as a comb.

Try this
You will need a plastic comb or pen, a wooly sweater, and tissue paper.

1 Tear off a few tiny pieces of tissue paper and put them on a table.

2 Rub the comb (or a pen) firmly on the sweater. Hold the comb near to the tissue paper.

Comb

Sweater

Tissue paper

3 The comb will pull the bits of tissue paper toward it. (If it doesn't, try rubbing the comb on the sweater again.)

It's a fact

The rubbing makes static electricity in the comb. The electricity can make things move.

ELECTRIC AMBER

An ancient Greek tried this experiment long ago. He found that if he rubbed **amber** on cat fur, the amber would then pull tiny objects toward it.

Amber

Static electricity can build up in a piece of amber.

Electric hair

You can use static electricity to make your hair stand on end!

Try this

To make your hair electric, you need a balloon.

1 Ask an adult to blow up the balloon and tie it closed. It is best if the balloon is very full of air.

2 Rub the balloon quickly up and down on your hair.

3 The rubbing makes static electricity collect in your hair. Your hair will start to stick up and out in all directions!

It works well if *your* hair is clean!

Sometimes pulling off a wooly hat can make your hair electric too!

It's a fact

As all the hairs become electric, they push away from each other. This makes them stand up and away from your head.

Spark in the dark

This experiment lets you make sparks! Static electricity can sometimes jump across a gap, making a spark.

Try this

You need a plastic comb and a wooly sweater. (You could use a plastic pen instead of a comb.)

1 Rub the comb hard and fast on the sweater to build up a lot of electricity in the comb.

2 Hold the comb close to a radiator or a metal sink faucet. Hold it as close as you can without touching.

Sweater

Comb

SUPERMARKET SHOCK

Static electricity can build up in shopping carts. When you touch them, the electricity jumps into you. It can give you a fright.

3 A tiny spark should jump across the gap. The spark is hard to see. But if you do the experiment in the dark, you might see it.

You might hear a tiny "click" when the spark jumps.

TAKE CARE not to bump into things if you do this experiment in the dark!

Glossary

Amber
Fossilized resin from trees that died long ago.

Appliance
A useful machine, such as a toaster. Electrical appliances run on electricity.

Battery
A container that stores electrical energy. When a battery is connected to a circuit, it releases electricity.

Contacts
Metal parts of a bulb, or other object, that can be connected to an electric circuit.

Electric current
A flow of electricity through a wire or other substance.

Energy
The power to make things work, happen, or move.

Socket
A device on a wall, through which you can connect an appliance to the electricity supply.

Static electricity
Electricity that builds up in an object, and does not flow.

Switch
A gap in a circuit. It can be closed to let electricity flow, or opened to stop the flow.

Terminals
Metal parts of a battery that can be connected to an electric circuit.

Turbine
A machine used in producing electricity. A turbine has blades that are turned by wind, steam, or water.

Index

Notes for parents and teachers

• These experiments use small batteries and amounts of electricity that cannot give a dangerous electric shock. Children must be reminded that electricity can be dangerous. Make sure they know not to play with electric sockets or plugs, make electrical items wet, or touch them with wet hands.

• Try counting all the electric lights you can find inside your home or school, including small on/off lights and indicator lights on appliances.

• Encourage children to learn to use everyday electrical items safely. Show them the switches on appliances such as phones and TVs, and let them see how they work.

• Lightning is a giant spark of static electricity. If you can do so safely, let children watch electrical storms with you and look out for lightning sparks. Talk about how lightning builds up in clouds, then jumps across the gap between the clouds and the ground.

• Let children watch you open up an electrical device such as a computer (though only do this if it is safe to do so according to the manufacturer). Show them the wires inside the machine and explain that electricity runs through the wires to make the machine work.

• Look out for electrical circuits and switches when you are out and about, and talk about how they might work. The button you press to stop traffic at a crosswalk is one example. Other examples are strings of Christmas lights, and automatic doors that open when you step on a mat.

• Point out overhead cables and pylons that carry electricity to houses and other buildings. Talk about where electricity comes from. It can be made by burning coal or oil in power stations, or from wind or water turning turbines.